River Map

River Map

JIM PERRIN

Photography by
JOHN BEATTY

First Impression—2001

ISBN 1 85902 996 5

© Text: Jim Perrin
© Photographs: John Beatty

Printed in Wales at
Gomer Press, Llandysul,
Ceredigion SA44 4QL

for Felicity
and in loving memory of
Barbara Mary Challoner

According to the legend, a dragon dredged the magical signs of the 'River Map' from a river. On it the sages discovered the drawing, and in the drawing the laws of the world-order.

C. G. Jung, *The Archetypes and the Collective Unconscious*

A pity beyond all telling
Is hid in the heart of love:
The folk who are buying and selling,
The clouds on their journey above,
The cold wet winds ever blowing,
And the shadowy hazel grove
Where mouse-grey waters are flowing,
Threaten the head that I love.

W. B. Yeats, *The Pity of Love*

The life in us is
like the water in
the river.

H. D. Thoreau, *Walden*

Contents

Prologue

To love another is to will what is really good for that person. Such love must be based on truth. A love that sees no distinction between good and evil, but loves blindly merely for the sake of loving, is hatred, rather than love. To love blindly is to love selfishly, because the goal of such love is not the real advantage of the beloved but only the exercise of love in our own souls.

Thomas Merton, *No Man Is An Island*

In the autumn of 1998 I returned to Wales after a long summer and fall spent travelling around the High Arctic and the Pacific North West of America. Through a series of synchronous events, I met and became involved with the most extraordinary, acutely intelligent, and to me entirely beautiful and loveable woman I had ever encountered. At the age that we were, and with the kind of history and experience we shared, it was inevitable that our relationship would prove difficult, on many occasions seem likely to end, and that its intensity – itself often a function of childhood experience – would further license difficulty to find expression within it.

The detail of all this is as affecting at times, as demeaning at other times, as the everyday emotional process of all our lives. Inevitably, this adds in its own charge, but it neither is nor should be any part of this book's explicit concern. Though what I give you here is travel-writing of a sort, its crucial theme – what this piece of writing is about at its most essential level – is the symbolic journey, the amelioristic impulse, the desire emotionally to move on and if possible to make good; or if not, if the obstacles without and within are too great, then at least to understand, with all the love, effort and forbearance that word implies; and to recognise that ultimately, under whatever duress, responsibility is always our own.

At one of the periods of breakdown between my companion and myself, something between a desire and the recognition of a necessity came upon me. I took it into my head to find my way to the source of the River Dee – incomparably the most beautiful of British rivers, and one that from childhood has held significance for me. As an admirer, albeit a sceptical one, of Jung's writings, I have a sense that these impulses are not accidental. It proved to be a path that took me through other planes than the simple, geographical one. The account I wrote of following its complex and turbulent course is, elliptically, crucially, a love letter to the woman to whom I have committed my life; and more obviously a celebration of a world I have been the more glad to inhabit through her presence in it.

Each of us, in our personal frame of morality, engages with the psychomachia – the battle between good and evil in our souls. Few, thank heavens, from determined weakness stay in thrall to the latter and are irrecoverably lost that way. We must all learn to live with choice, error and consequence. Through a wise and discerning acceptance of this, and through good faith, we can perhaps hope to reach the pure springs beyond polluted motive, response and action. This is the theme stitched into this book through a sub-textual study of the psychological dimension of landscape, and an account of an individual progress to recognition of the need for attentiveness in all areas of life: not just to one's own hurt and need, one's own feelings of pain, anger, rejection and abandonment, but to those of others; not just to the pollution without, but to that which clouds and taints our vision from within; not just to the personal and internal – the solipsistic landscape, but to the actual and objective one too, that reflects, and can teach. For which reason, though my heart may have been fixed on a remoter object in the course of this source-quest, eye and mind were concerned to register and express all the exquisite, bright texture of the natural world, all there that delights, and our responsibility to its preservation.

Here then is a River Map, and in it a real journey that perhaps brought real possibility of change. It brought me back from weariness, intense hurt and despair to an appreciation of the beauty of the world, and of one exceptional, rigorously challenging, lovely, hopeful, defended and vulnerable woman within it. Let others follow their own journeys along the course of the River Dee, the Afon Dyfrdwy, if they will, and from whatever perspectives they may. Let them, as I hope they will, enjoy it, and all its manifold gifts to their appreciative consciousness along the paths they take by its course.

And if, finally, you press me once again to answer that question as to what River Map is about, I would want to respond with this perception. However pleasurable or desirable this may be, it is not a rewarding connection with the object of one's love that is crucial, but the flow of love itself, its purity, its constancy, its holding to the channel it has chosen in hope of attaining for its object the good of the other. If this spring can be tapped within, all contingent issue that muddies its current ultimately, surely, can be cleansed and washed away?

If we only knew, if we could only learn how . . .

Jim Perrin,
Y Waun,
July 2001

February: an ending or a beginning?

. . . faith belongs to and has its home in the existential, and in all eternity it has nothing to do with knowledge as a comparative or superlative.

Søren Kierkegaard, *Journals 1853-1855*

The best and worst of things in our lives begin on impulse. Though maybe it's not impulse at all, just a subtle predisposition, a tilt in the strata of feeling that inclines us in one direction; so that as we drift and dream along, suddenly impetus itself carries us down a steepening slope towards a widening gap. An emotional groundwork precedes all our actions, gives them a momentum by which we are often surprised.

I want to tell you of a journey, made over a period of months. Perhaps it is one that all of you who read this narrative will have followed – at some level, in one dimension or another? For although it was a physical journey, that began in one place and may have ended in another, it was also a path taken out of a period of confusion and anguish in my life, that led ultimately into a better state of being, a clearer sense of my loved one, myself and the world. So the following of this course, the traverse of this landscape, was a form of therapy – of retrieval and re-affirmation – as well as a process of actual discovery.

Throughout one bitter personal winter, I'd been spending time around the spoiled splendour of the Dee estuary. At the ebb of the tide I'd crossed the sand to the wildlife sanctuary of Hilbre Island, that lies cheek by jowl with the most jostling of Wirral suburbia but is a place apart. My companion and I had walked along the saltings from Parkgate, on old sandstone wharves grooved by mooring ropes that sawed down into the soft, red, pebbly rock on flowing tides of centuries ago. None of the bustle of unloading, the relief, fatigue or excitement of the fishermen's return, is to be heard there now. Nor is it entirely quiet. A dramatic, shrill sunset dyed the clouds bloody and intense over the hills of Wales. Geese were restive and clamorous among the marshes. In counterpoint, a sentimental ballad from Charles Kingsley's novel *Alton Locke* was running over and over in my mind:

> Oh Mary, go and call the cattle home,
> And call the cattle home,
> And call the cattle home
> Across the sands of Dee;
> The western wind was wild and dank with foam.
> And all along went she.
>
> The western tide crept up along the sand,
> And o'er and o'er the sand,
> And round and round the sand,
> As far as eye could see.
> The rolling mist came down and hid the land:
> And never home came she.

I was remembering reading it years ago through a long, sunlit day spent lounging alone in silky *machair* on the west coast of Iona. Encounters with books and with music are surely things that enrich, and are enriched by, their time and place. I remember so exactly when I first read or heard so many favourite things: William Blake in a basement flat on the Seven Sisters Road, Rilke on Ynys Enlli, *Sir Gawain and the Green Knight* in a Herefordshire orchard one autumn evening over thirty years ago; Kathleen Ferrier's performance of the *Abschied* from *Das Lied von der Erde*, Bob Dylan singing *It's Alright Ma, I'm Only Bleeding*, or Bach's cantata *Wachet auf* – all this glowing, rich texture that brings resonance and a deeper understanding to our lives. But I was living through a phase without literature, music, or reflective, quiet thought; my companion and I were in bitter conflict. Tensions and

vulnerabilities had compounded in our life together. There was a need upon us to disengage, in order to move beyond our difficulties and perhaps eventually find each other again.

So you see, in my own mind I was at an ending – of a river, of a phase in my life. That useful construct of T. S. Eliot's, the 'objective correlative', was crowding in on me down here among the spilling bleak where fresh drowns in salt to begin its cycle all over again. We seek out these places at these times for a reason that's often well concealed and deep within. And when we have done so, and find our inner landscape reflected in them, choice emerges, objectified. Do we submit to mergence, our individualities extinguished by it? Should we allow that? Is it a gate by which power and its close cousin malignity come in?

There is a canalised cut that takes the Dee down from its last rock bluffs and meanders across the dreariest of industrial landscapes to this loss of identity, this sea-change. Let's skip a few miles and a period of time, because I do not wish to impose any more than is necessary of that desperate landscape upon you.

On a temporarily sunny February weekday lunchtime, with the companion from whose *Way* mine was then divergent, and a brightness of day and future quavering and unconvinced above us, I was in a restaurant on Lower Bridge Street in Chester – Chester, where the ineffably decent Charles Kingsley was Canon; Chester, where in the summer of 1854 George Borrow began his journey into Wales that he shaped into the finest of all travel books set in these islands; Chester, where the alien legionaries gazed with suspicion and anxiety across the Dee marshes into the hills of Wales. My companion and I had often walked the circuit of the city walls here together, and I had hoped we would walk it hand-in-hand and happily again.

From the pavement outside this restaurant on Lower Bridge Street, I used to catch the green Crosville double-decker bus to Llangollen as a boy of thirteen or so at the outset of all my early lone journeys into Wales. I remember being on that bus, on the front seat upstairs as it lurched and groaned its way through Gresford and Wrexham, Johnstown and Ruabon, and all the way I was barely able to sit still with the excitement of seeing hills – the same hills my grandparents had left fifty years before – rising to the west.

Today in the restaurant I was dreaming, as usual – this time about Borges's idea: that all the great metaphors have already been expressed, and that the writer can only hope to re-inform them through personal experience; and also I was thinking about my friend the Gaelic poet Cathal O'Searcaigh's insistence, in his poem *An Tobar* ('The Well'), on this perhaps cruel necessity:

> Seek out your own well, my dear,
> For the age of want is near:
> There will have to be a going back to sources.

Then the impulse came to me, the sudden inclination to run with it, to take a particular direction in life. The weir, that marks an ambiguous but satisfying boundary between riverine and estuarine, was by the bridge a couple of hundred yards down the road. From it, the Dee's course stretched up to its springs and source high among the loneliest and to me most-loved group of Welsh mountains. I scarcely knew, in that precise detail which is the only meaningful way to encounter landscape, what happened along the way. But I would find out. And I would begin now.

'Darling,' I said to my companion, because however things are going, and however sharp and frequent the refusal of them, it is important at these times to offer reassurance and connection, 'I'm going to walk upriver. I'll find a pub at nightfall and ring you from there, in case you want to come out and meet me.'

She raised her eyebrows, took the car keys from me, shook her head at the vagaries of men. A few minutes later, dressed in city clothes, with a small green woman's umbrella tucked at her sensible and considerate urging into the pocket of my overcoat, I was ambling along the river bank and leaving life's ordinaries and real or imagined restrictions rapidly behind.

Have you been to Budapest or Varanasi? They are shrines to the oldest gods. Rivers and cities exist always in uneasy conjunction – the latter like spectators at a circus when the lion tamer plies his trade. They shrink back, climb the banks, keep their safe and respectful distances. There is recognition always of what might happen if the beast is loosed. All the way along the King's Meadow, round Earl's Eye, through Queen's Park, you meet with a sense of civilisation cautiously, politely witnessing its own penetration by the wild, attempting absurdly to match the elemental by naming in the most potent of its own degrees. Until quite suddenly, straggling houses above the flood-plain fade on either side; you circumvent fields of placid bulls, pass beneath the concrete bridge of the bypass, and are freed to nature's proper tangle and confusion.

Down on the estuary, biting unfettered winds assert the season's drabness. 'Not yet spring' is their refrain, and it keeps the listening grasses to a grey complexion. But along the sheltered banks and in the secret woods, snowdrops drift waxy-white in profusion, the broad-bladed leaves of ramson – beautiful, starry-flowered, triangular-stemmed wild woodland garlic – are cutting through the loam, uncurling, and from an occasional sun-aligned ditch-side the first celandine flowers blink. Dusty hazel catkins shake and catch at fitful shafts of light. Gem-like unfolding green buds stud the armed and contorted branches of the blackthorns. This is the very brink of seasonal change, spring rousing out of the dead time, flexing its muscles, making ready, and the evidence of this process of renewal brings with it a curious intimation of joy, so seldom accessible in the city down there.

Somewhere beyond Eccleston, after negotiating a self-consciously charming stretch of riverside path with steps and crannies and grottoes in the exposed sandstone, I sat very quietly on a fence to watch the brown, rippling flow of the river, and doing so made me peaceful and rather happy. The surface was suddenly broken. Ten feet away, low in the water, was a cormorant. The bird held a silver fish maybe six inches in length crosswise in its long beak, tossed it up and swallowed it with a long spasm of the throat, then dived again. A little farther, in the mud by a shallow eddy, were an otter's distinctive five-toed prints. Passing through this landscape there came a recurrent strong sense that I might observe, and receive gifts here and there – that flash of irridescence was surely a kingfisher, a bird I had not seen for twenty years – but the more acute watchers stay well hidden and wary, and the riverbank protects and conceals them, is known and accessible to them in a way that it never will be to me.

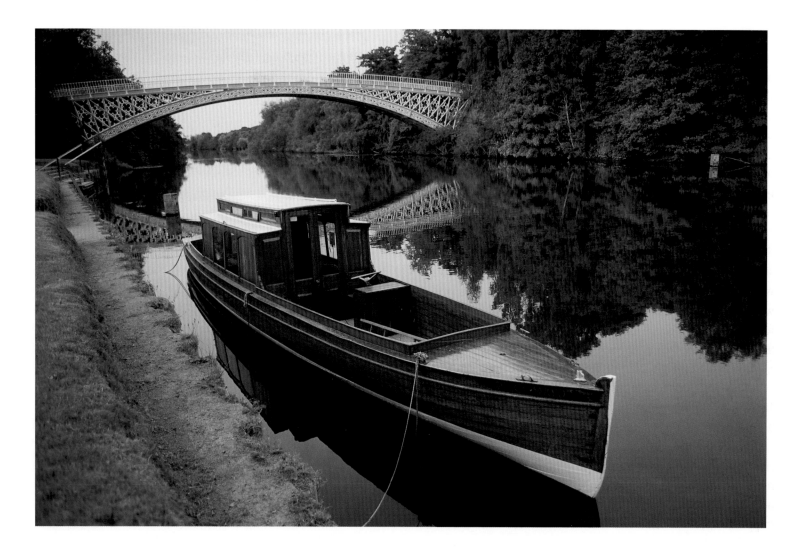

That sense grew, and also an empathic knowledge: that the wariness of the unseen creatures observing my passage here was justified, an apt response to what Thomas Merton calls 'the wound in our nature'. Despite which, I fell into a *Wind in the Willows* reverie, tumbled headlong into the trap of sentimentality. Here was Mole, lost in the Wild Wood, starting at every movement and sound, fierce wedge-shaped faces with their glittering eyes watching him. I crossed the river by the Iron Bridge on the Buerton approach to the Duke of Westminster's seat at Eaton Hall, and the vision vanished.

The elegance of the bridge was outlined in blue paint too disconsonantly bright on a cloudy February afternoon for muted surroundings. An impression of lightness about it belied the weight of its ironwork. At the lodge house and kennels on the west bank a half-dozen assorted terriers issued out to scold me for my presence there. I leant over the parapet and talked back to them as they sat sturdy and attentive with cocked heads, hearing me out. Their mannerisms reminded me unbearably of my own constant companion over seventeen years, The Flea – a little Jack Russell terrier, full of character and fun, who'd died a year before. I cried a little at her memory, and carried on.

A brief diversion by muddy pathways that led away from the riverbank took me past a striking medieval motte with a deep moat around it and into the estate village of Aldford, where the houses are absurdly neat and ornate in their brickwork, but their trappings speak of tenancies and poor pay. The village church is

large, drab, and astonishingly ugly, and the reek of feudalism hung on the air and rose thin and acrid from every decorative chimney-stack. This, after all, is Cheshire of the great estates. I resisted the urge to tug my forelock and hurried on, regaining the river where it curves away into a great meander that put me in mind of school geography lessons. So this was the mature phase? Well – even objective correlatives have their limitations.

Pairs of mallard flew off noisily from oxbow lakes beyond the farther bank. From little square enclosures of non-native trees – Jones' Wood, Speed's Plantation, Sourbutt's Covert (this whole landscape is apostrophised by ownership) – came the echoing poom! of guns. This is what a particular faction likes to call 'sporting' country. The men – they're all that, for this debased and vile activity is no more than sadistically substitutive ejaculation – were shooting wood-pigeons and rooks, *corvids* they term the latter in their own press, to give an air of spurious scientific justification to their bloodlust. And there's no rook pie on their menus. They don't eat what they kill, as country people did a hundred years ago, in Richard Jefferies' time. They do it for the sub-human pleasures of cruelty and the exercise of power. I moved on, a little sickened by my own gender and species.

In Waterstone's Bookshop in Chester before setting out, I'd bought a map – the 1:25,000 Pathfinder sheet for this stretch of river. On it, the riverbank stretches empty right down to Farndon and Holt. But on the ground, it's otherwise. A dense river-bank settlement appeared. Every fifty yards or less was some makeshift, rickety, gimcrack habitation hammered together from boards and fretted sheets of ply and corrugated iron and scaffolding tube, and each had its quota of locks and barbed wire and lichenous, waterlogged pram dinghies and hopeful grand nomenclature: Bank House, Mon Repos, The Cottage, Stepaside, Walden (yes, *Walden*! That amiable man and great naturalist William Condry told me, only half in jest, that he slept all his life with a copy under his pillow. Do people still read Thoreau? For so many reasons I hope they do.) The paint of these sixty- or seventy-year old huts and chalets peels, the wood rots, supports sag into riparian clay.

Most are deserted, although beneath one a couple of men were excavating a deep hole.

'What are you doing?' I asked.

A mud-streaked, good-humoured face peered out and grinned. 'Burying the wife,' he replied.

A footpath sign told that it was three kilometres to Farndon, and eleven back to Chester. The rain had set in, obscuring the hills of Denbighshire over to the west beyond the geographical remnants of Cheshire's wealth-creating plain. The national border between Wales and England slipped into the Dee along Pulford Brook, so that the far bank was now another country across rain-stippled and rippling water. I took the umbrella from my pocket, hunched in behind it, and splashed on through the mire. Little red cliffs of triassic rock, black ooze seeping from their bedding planes, bulbous-rooted oaks grasping their crowns, walled the path. At dusk, lights glimmered through the downpour in the village of Farndon, from which I crossed into Holt and Wales. In the Gredington Arms on the village green they lit for me a living-flame fire and pulled me a pint of bland, palatable beer with not enough substance for George Borrow's taste (*Wild Wales* is full of panegyrics on or fulminations against the variable quality of the Welsh nation's beer). I rang my companion, extracted a novel from an inner pocket of my sodden overcoat, eased into a deep sofa, trousers steaming from the heat of the fire, and promptly fell into deep and dreamless sleep. If anyone noticed, nobody minded, and I was only aroused by the arrival, perhaps an hour later, of my companion.

March: 'The land that is afar off'

On leaving Holt, I returned over the bridge; and, passing along a portion of CHESHIRE, in a flat country, with a pleasing view of the Broxton hills on the left, I reached the site of Shocklach castle.

Thomas Pennant, *A Tour in Wales (1778-1783)*

Thomas Pennant is the most endearing and knowledgeable of travellers. Reading *A Tour in Wales*, it's easy to understand why Gilbert White chose him for a correspondent. (*The Natural History of Selborne*, our best-loved classic of nature writing, is in the form of letters addressed to Pennant.) But for all his habitual good humour, something got under Pennant's skin in Holt. He didn't choose to linger there, and nor did I.

Holt is famous for having formerly possessed one of the most imposing of all the Marcher castles. Detailed plans and illustrations of it exist in the Bodleian Library, and if you're lucky enough to possess a copy of the *Tour in Wales* you can see them copied there. But there's not much left of the castle on the ground, other than the gloomy, litter-infested quarry-moat from which its masonry came. That masonry was taken downriver by a later band of robbers in the 1870s to help build the residence of the Dukes of Westminster at Eaton Hall. Nowadays the best feature of this ancient settlement on the Welsh side of the Dee is the coffee-house on The Cross, which might tempt the foot-traveller to stay if he or she were not mindful of how much time it can take to follow the minutiae of footpaths through agricultural country as they are marked on 1:25,000 maps. In my case, this process involves much doffing of distance spectacles and fumbling to find reading glasses, and then the right map, because this is one of those areas where endless sheets converge. I sometimes think the reason I like mountains best is because there the objectives are so plain. On high hills you can rely on acquired mountain sense, read the ground and do away with the map, which is anyway best read indoors, where it becomes a fascinating speculative text in its own right. With these complex footpath sequences, I always feel like some bleary academic squinting his way through page after page of six-point footnotes: 'So I should be heading at about thirty degrees from that hedge towards . . . right! There's a stile'. You become so engrossed in finding where you are, that you lose sight of where you are, and more especially of what's around you.

All this seems both relevant and historically dissonant in Holt, for these twin villages of Farndon and Holt, on either side of the river, were the childhood home of the Elizabethan cartographer John Speed, whose fascination with 'the land that is afar off' reputedly derived from looking out to the surrounding hills from one or other of the church towers, and wondering how landscape might best be drawn. But my argument's not with him, whose preoccupation in a sense I share, and of whose maps the kindest description might be that they are impressionistic. I spent a fortnight sharing a tent in Kirgizstan once with a man from the Ordnance Survey. He was a pleasant man in his way, and I would generally as soon read a map as a book; but there is a colonial cast of mind among these people that is not mine. Brian Friel's *Translations* is the appropriate text to read here.

Pennant, to come back to him, was remarkably uneasy in Holt, and commented with unusual acerbity on the effects of Owain Glyndŵr's insurrection at the beginning of the fifteenth century on the place:

> This instilled into the inhabitants a spirit, retained, perhaps, to this moment; for within these few years they were the most irascible and pugnacious of all the neighbourhood.

That temper of the town probably pre-dates Glyndŵr. A century before his time, in the Welsh Wars of Edward I, this area had been known as the King's Marsh – the name still exists as that of a civil parish – and it had been settled by outlaws and brigands who were offered sanctuary here from the law in return for serving the king against the depredations of the Welsh. Maybe future medico-criminologists will dig up the churchyards of Farndon and Holt and do DNA tests on bones from early graves to determine whether there is a psychopathic or outlaw gene? If you're at all historically minded, then the leaving of Holt is fraught with psychic danger. There is a small matter of a Welsh version of the Princes in the Tower, reputed murdered here by being drowned in the river at the command of their rapacious Marcher Lord guardians; so that if you leave Holt over the sturdy cutwaters of the fourteenth-century bridge that crosses to Farndon, and it is night, and you're on horseback, well . . .

> Belated travellers quake with fear,
> And spur their starting horse;
> For childish shrieks they say they hear,
> As Farndon's bridge they cross.

It was broad daylight and I was on foot, so I was subjected to no such discomfiting experience. But like Pennant, all I choose to recall about the country beyond, along the east bank of the Dee between here and Shocklach, is that it is 'a flat country'. It's beautiful enough, in a kempt, lowland style, this Vale of Maelor. It feels like Cheshire, to which a few miles of the east bank of the Dee still belong before the Welsh border throws out the disconnected historical curiosity of a long salient towards Whitchurch that's called – for very good reason these days – the English Maelor.

I had an objective for the afternoon, which was Overton, ten or twelve miles upstream. A progression of footpaths clearly marked on the map led to it. Cheshire is heavily committed in the direction of its footpaths. There is the Marches Way, and there is the Maelor Way, and there are many other ways no doubt, of which I remain blissfully unaware. I went down one day to the tourist centre in Chester specifically to ask for information on them, but they could provide me with none. If I'd wanted a reservation for bed-and-breakfast in Llandudno or Lismahagow, that they could have managed, which says a lot about modern tourism; but on these ways of theirs, not a pamphlet or a word.

So to them I added the way that I went – which may well have coincided with the ways they no doubt admirably somewhere describe, and in the field even intermittently signpost. This way of mine, and probably theirs too, though I have no certain knowledge of this, led me out of curiosity and by way of a slight detour to a little bluff above the river, where there was a church insignificantly marked. And I'm extremely glad that I chanced upon it.

Church-going may be in sad decline, but church-visiting still seems to me one of the pleasantest and most civilised of pursuits. The best churches have a gathered and time-burnished appropriateness and aspiring that in some subtle and subliminal way brings spiritual comfort. And they need not be grand. When

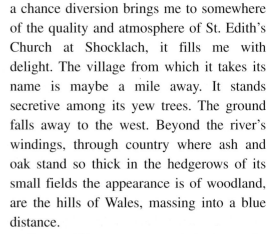

a chance diversion brings me to somewhere of the quality and atmosphere of St. Edith's Church at Shocklach, it fills me with delight. The village from which it takes its name is maybe a mile away. It stands secretive among its yew trees. The ground falls away to the west. Beyond the river's windings, through country where ash and oak stand so thick in the hedgerows of its small fields the appearance is of woodland, are the hills of Wales, massing into a blue distance.

The twelfth-century church is tiny, built of a warm red sandstone the blocks of which have weathered pillowy with age. The south door is a carved Romanesque arch (its decorative motifs of chevron and cable markedly similar to those at the magnificent Wenlock Priory forty miles to the south), and the building reveals all those little organic changes of the centuries clearly in its fabric. In the carefully-tended churchyard is the broken shaft of a Norman cross. Rabbits burrow around thick-slabbed gravestones that have delaminated into illegibility; a chestnut tree buds plump and pale against a wash of sky; rooks and stock-doves chorus the place.

Even without the detail of knowledge, the story here reads plain. Unlike Holt, St. Edith's churchyard does tempt you to linger. I did. An old countryman arrived as I sat on the grass. His dog, a tiny, dock-tailed, young Jack Russell with a comical black-and-tan mask, ran up to me, rolled over submissively for me to scratch his belly, jumped up and licked my ears. 'Oh, Sam adores everyone, and they adore him,' his owner told me. He was Mr. Evans and he lived in the village, walked here every day. They were having trouble in the churchyard with the crows, that were stealing flowers from the graves to line their nests. But they wouldn't be shooting them – oh no! Maybe the schoolchildren would come out and make a scarecrow or two. He'd been baptised here in St. Edith's sixty-six years ago. Local, then? Well, not really – his family came from Montgomeryshire. But his mother and father were buried here, just over on that side, and he'd be joining them one day. 'Come on then, Sam,' he called, 'time for your dinner. I buys him a chicken once or twice a week,' he confided, 'cooks it for him and he likes that. Not the bones, mind – I don't give him the bones.'

Away they went, the little dog scampering in tight, listing circles around his master, who conversed fondly with him all the while. Time had passed, the sun had wheeled round noticeably on its course so I roused myself to ramble on through pleasant meadows, Wrexham industry conspicuous beyond the farther bank of the river. Months later a discharge, perhaps accidental, was to poison these lower stretches of the river, killing all the fish, rendering it lifeless, some experts think, for the next twenty years. I thought, when I heard, of kingfisher, otter and cormorant; and of how physical pollution has its psychological counterparts in our lives – its corresponding, learnt or inherited manifestations of instability, cruelty, rage and avarice, from the effects of which regeneration is equally difficult and long, if achievable at all.

Somewhere along the line of a weedy little brook unnamed on the map but called, according to Pennant, the Flannen, I crossed back into Wales and soon found myself in the straggling village of Worthenbury. With the excuse of having the Borrovian spirit on me again, I went looking for – and found – beer, in a pub where the girth of the landlord spoke of his pleasure in it too. It was good enough, but not the best beer I ever tasted. That was in a stone-flagged pub on Swan Hill in Shrewsbury nearly thirty years ago. It was drawn from barrels behind a rough wooden bar, was flat, amber-coloured, almost viscous in consistency, and the taste was so rich and strong it lingers on my palate still and my head spins a little when I think of it. I went back a year or two later. The beer had been casked and carbonated, the pub thematised, and a briskly efficient manager installed who explained dismissively the non-cost-effectiveness and temperamentality of barrelled beers. Maybe it has changed again since his time.

In Worthenbury I also found another church. Pennant mentions it as 'a new and neat building dedicated to St. Deiniol'. It had been built forty years before his visit here – between 1736 and 1739 – by a Staffordshire stonemason and architect, Richard Trubshaw, an interesting and gifted character who was also a champion wrestler (his grandson James was one of the most versatile and successful engineers and architects at the end of that century, and had thrown the triumphal single-stone-arched bridge over the Dee at Chester against Telford's predictions of impossibility) .

St. Deiniol's Church is quite unlike St. Edith's, but if anything it is even more fascinating. Its glowing redbrick, pale ashlar coigns, its serene churchyard and its stately tower with a weathervane at each corner are all wonderfully pleasing and harmonious. To step inside is to step straight back into the eighteenth century. There's an organ loft, box pews and chancel pews with little fireplaces to keep the gentry warm through the long winter services. Some of the glass in the East Window is far older than the church itself. It actually dates from the fourteenth century, was more or less filched by a restorers' workshop in Shrewsbury during an early nineteenth-century restoration of Winchester College Chapel, and re-deployed here. The effect of St. Deiniol's whole interior is luminously and gracefully of its period of order, harmony and the light of reason. It calmed me, and I resolved to bring my companion here one day.

Shadows of tall trees were stretching across the churchyard as I hurried back down towards the river and along to Bangor-is-y-Coed. This, to pick up on the religious theme, was formerly one of the great ecclesiastical sites in Britain. Pelagius of heretical fame – he who so unreasonably, by the lights of the early church fathers in Rome, disputed the doctrine of original sin, believed unbaptised infants to be safe from damnation, and thought good works in themselves meritorious – was a monk here, and one whose presence was in part responsible for schism from Rome, and dire consequence. For somewhere near Bangor was the

scene, in 613 A.D., of a massacre of monks prompted, if the Venerable Bede is to be believed, by St. Augustine:

> [The British Bishops refused to] recognize Augustine as their archbishop, saying among themselves that if he would not rise to greet them in the first instance, he would have even less regard for them once they submitted to his authority. Whereupon Augustine, that man of God, is said to have answered with a threat that was also a prophecy: if they refused to accept peace with their fellow-Christians, they would be forced to accept war at the hands of enemies; and if they refused to preach to the English the way of life, they would eventually suffer at their hands the penalty of death. And, by divine judgement, all these things happened as Augustine foretold.

Consider that 'by divine judgement'. As Kierkegaard notes in a different context, 'Augustine has done incalculable harm'. Our British Christianity would have had an entirely different cast had he not set foot on these islands. But authority secures its own profit, gets away with what it will, and presents its own agreed versions to posterity. After the slaughter, the few survivors fled from here either to Basingwerk Abbey on the estuary of the Dee, or through the Welsh mountains to Ynys Enlli – lonely little wild Bardsey, the island off the tip of the Llŷn Peninsula, where they established the most remote of Welsh monastic settlements. I had some fellow-feeling for them, looking upriver into the hills. Perhaps that way civilised and unpolluting responses between

human beings might still lie, I found myself hoping; and that was the way, ultimately, that I was bound. Nowadays Bangor-on-Dee, as it's usually called, is best known for its racecourse, beautifully situated in a crook of the river, where I might have felt inclined to place a bet, but the next meeting was in a week's time. So instead I hurried on to Overton, on the leisurely, wide main street of which the White Lion promised affable, noisy company.

'How're you doing?' I offered to the woman on a stool next to me at the bar, who was giving me an amused, see-what-the-wind's-blown-in smile.

'I'm very happy, thanks,' she replied.

'So what's the secret?'

'Oh, I'll tell you that,' she came back, full of spark, a gorgeous young girl of eight or so who was obviously her daughter butting in to her armpit shyly, 'I wake up each morning, open the window, look out, and the birds are singing. That's all. Try it.'

April: Rights of Passage

. . . before the soul,
Which now is mine, must re-attain
Immunity from my control,
And wander round the world again;

Before this teas'd o'erlaboured heart
For ever leaves its vain employ,
Dead to its deep habitual smart,
And dead to hopes of future joy.

Matthew Arnold, *The River*

The River Dee at Overton swills out suddenly from between the jaws of the hills. Thereafter it describes leisurely arcs across the plain, losing barely a metre in height for every mile of the remaining twenty in its course to the sea. But above Overton, it starts to take on an urgency and a vigour, its current grows rapid, its surface is flecked with white. For about six miles, too, along a tortuous escape course, it becomes secretive, invisible from roads, and for one stretch of perhaps two miles in length, surprisingly difficult of access. For me, much of this was unexplored country.

So one bright Sunday morning early in April, the photographer John Beatty and myself set off from Overton to walk upriver to Llangollen. John is one of my closest friends and an exhilarating walking companion, all dash and flair and madcap, intense enthusiasm, full of stories and plans and chatter to while away any mile that might threaten to become tedious. I tell him he's crazy, which to old hippies and Sixties-survivors, as some might think we are, is just an endorsing Laingian code – craziness as a mode of sanity in a mad world. It's a view that tempts me, and more often than from time to time. Craziness as light-filled, questing energy, as a form of genius leagues away from the dark, grasping psychoses that conceal themselves so easily and respectably among the mores of contemporary society? Maybe . . . and

certainly, I'd rather John's brand of craziness than many people's versions of sanity.

John, too, was off his home patch – in his case the Dark Peak moorland of Derbyshire – so in consequence was sparking away with an eager, zestful curiosity. We bustled out of Overton's quiet main street – like many of the villages in this part of the

Welsh Marches it feels like some little, towny remnant of the eighteenth century from which the tide of progress has long receded – along the Wrexham road, and in a quarter-mile or so, out of simple nosiness, dipped through a gated and dilapidated entrance just beyond a public footpath sign to discover a lich-gate, house martins' nests in its eaves, in the trees behind.

'St. Mary's churchyard', read a sign. 'Part of this graveyard is being allowed to revert to a wildflower meadow. Please respect it.'

On its farther side, the lich-gate gave on to a long, sunny terrace, more terraces below it and a roofless, vandalised chapel at its farther end. On the steps down to the chapel, local cannabis-smoking contemplatives had left evidence of their activity. They can have few better places for it.

The river, still visible through budded spring branches, curved away beneath to the south and west, into the hills, promising and alluring, but in this lost garden of graves all future dimension was absent.

It had become one of the accomplished places where time is a thing of sun and season alone. The chiffchaff sings its repetitive song, the primroses crowd banks above rows of tombs in littery profusion. The atmosphere is entirely Victorian. Heighten the colours or add a mysterious, gracefully-draped female figure here and there and it would be perfectly in the spirit of a Millais painting or a Julia Margaret Cameron photograph. Its going back, re-absorbing, puts me precisely in mind of the opening lines of Tennyson's 'Tithonus', to whose age it so completely belongs:

The woods decay, the woods decay and fall,
And after many a summer dies the swan.

Reunited with my companion, I came back here later, in the green time of year, to show it to her. We sat side by side on the

steps behind the church under a hot afternoon sun, an unspoken excitement pulsing between us. She tugged at my coat, pulled it from my shoulders, laid it beneath her on the stone flags. Much later, across the peace of afterwards, a plane flew overhead. She shoved me off into young nettles and we, sky-clad in the garden, struggled back into the world of concealment. The surge of desire stilled down to a deep, rippling intimacy that lasted throughout that day and the next, the river flowing through us, intermingling.

Today, John and I left the churchyard behind, induced by it into rather a dreamy mood, and descended through woods bright with blossom and with evidence all around of badger activity, to join the riverbank among meadows. Within half a mile the south bank was becoming steep and craggy and the path ran through oak woodland, the trees gnarled and mossy, the ground under them starred with wood anemones in great drifts, and leaf and stem of bluebells scything up in readiness for that magical displacement to a shimmer of blue as April progresses. This stretch of the river is particularly beautiful. It is here that it makes its true exit from the hills, eases down into eddying, slow reaches in the shadowy depths of which it's easy to imagine pike lurking rapacious as freshwater sharks, or trout of immense age and girth, and salmon too in their season, like characters in stories from the Welsh oral tradition, able to differentiate between a mayfly hatch and the angler's lure, able suddenly to surface and converse with passing humans, to dispense their oracular and magically acquired wisdom and salve, to use Thomas Merton's phrase again, 'the wound in our nature'.

On the opposite bank is a gloomy, small church and a little settlement, of cottages and riverside pub, skeins of blue smoke winding from their chimneys. It's called Erbistock. The pub is The Boat, and is much in demand for marriages. Its prettiness might well lure an unwitting man or woman into those celebrations that can precede difficulty or even disaster. They might glimpse a chimera upon those sloping lawns, prancing around the promise of happiness, pursue and find a changeling there. Or they might, pray heaven, after long struggle reach the good. How are we to know what rocks or rapids will roughen and divide the flow of our feelings, or what poisons can spill in from the sullied tributaries of our own or others' lives? *How do we find our way back to the pure springs*?

The river was swollen, the marked ford over to its cold north bank impassable, so we carried on with a shudder, no drinks for us at that source. The path along the bank led past craglets and rock shelters of a soft and blocky sandstone, and over footbridges spanning confluent streams where splay-footed otter tracks, and those of badger too, were distinct in silty red flats where they joined the river. I love this grace that animals can accord us, this evidence of things unseen, these indications of presences that make more complete our understanding of the scene. Between ourselves as humans, fragmented by the demands and abuses of the world, we are able – for whatever

ambition we desire to promote – to disguise and dissemble about our true nature; but the animal world doesn't thus deceive, gives its clues honestly to our perceptive consciousness. Surely thus it should receive in return our unconditional love? As if to underline that message, from the under-bank a pair of red-breasted mergansers took off and skidded noisily away, crossing the water, leaving the river.

Soon we took our cue from them, and followed a lane southwards, forking from it down a mirey sunken way that led parallel to the Dee and was bordered with primroses and violets. As it descended the hill, its muddiness intensified to a state of over-the-tops-of-boots, cattle-trampled quagmire. We opted for the field alongside, where the coconut scent of gorse, in flower and sun-warmed, permeated the air so strongly we sat down just to drink it in, and having done so, opened our flasks as well and looked around us. To the west the limestone escarpments ringed Eglwyseg Mountain, and the wood-pulp mill at Chirk sent a plume of smoke into the sky, reminding us how close to industry we were even in this quietly ravishing version of field-and-woodland-and-glittering-river British pastoral. Local in its scale, it's as lovely as anything you encounter on the Offa's Dyke Path, that passes by four miles to the west, and feels the tramp of tens of thousands of feet every year. I doubt if more than a few dozen walkers come this way in the same space of time. That supposition was certainly borne out when we passed beyond the confluence pool of the Dee and the Afon Ceiriog.

The latter is one of the most beautiful of Welsh rivers, and the place where it joins the Dee is one to linger at and rejoice in. Its banks writhe with the exposed roots of old trees, the new-partnering rivers swirl together in an easy waltz. Fishermen, with whom the place must be popular, seem to appreciate it. On the far bank is a simple shelter that you could imagine some latter-day Izaak Walton occupying for the length of a summer's day, watching the eddies under the slow search of the sun. For John and myself there was a more arduous experience in store. I'd been tempted to follow the Ceiriog up to its waterfall-jewelled head in the Berwyn moorland, and then to cross by one of the old passes to the Dee again at Cynwyd or Llandrillo. But that was known country, and too recently and painfully associative for me. Ahead of us on our river was a hidden stretch, of which I knew nothing, and to traverse which would be personal discovery.

It began well enough. There were meadows, fishermen's benches, the river sweeping by, more mergansers clattering away urgently upstream. A boundary fence or two had to be crossed, but there was no sense of threat about them, none of the habitual signed prohibition. That was reserved for former Wynnstay land over on the opposite bank – once the heart of the largest estate in Wales, presided over by successive Sir Watkins Williams Wynnes who were generally and jocularly referred to as the kings of Wales. On the strength of a few 'Private' notices we spied over there, I mouthed quietly one of my favourite imprecations, from Gerrard Winstanley, the Diggers' leader from the time of the English Revolution, against all such places. It runs like this:

> Was the Earth made to preserve a few covetous proud men to live at ease, and for them to bag and barn up the treasures of the Earth from others that these may beg and starve in a fruitful land; or was it made to preserve all her children?

I was soon to recant. The Sir Watkins, by most contemporary accounts, were fair and generous landlords, and concerned for the wellbeing of people and land. The patch of earth that we were now crossing had need of an attitude like that. It had been planted with conifers, and these had been clear-felled. The ground lay about us in ruins, drainage ditches clogged, brushwood choking any new growth, its wealth dragged away. The Earth is a finite resource. It is all we have. No one has the right to treat it thus. The tax-concessioned, money-fixated speculators who do so only see the cash their accountants tell them they gain, not the effect they have on the landscape and their responsibility for that. If they did, would they care? If we do not treat the land well on which we live, if we are thus obsessed by personal gain at the cost of a universal morality, can we hope truly to do well by the people with whom we live? I do not think so, am personally aware how easily, at how little negative stimulus, I can fall for whatever period from good intent. For two miles, along what must, thirty years ago, have been a dramatic and idyllic stretch of river, there was now desolation and hard-going to be endured. No birds flew. The river ran deep, fast and dark. This place that no one now knows was eerily and unnaturally lifeless, soundless, as though withdrawing into itself from the abuse committed upon it.

We escaped up a pathway through more badger-haunted woods – tidy little dung-filled pits of their toilet along the margin of the trees – to Pentre, a neat estate village, cared-for and friendly, and from it crossed the road to gain the towpath of the Shropshire Union Canal. In doing so we'd missed out a contorted long bend of the Dee around a spur pocked with old workings that are being used as a landfill site, but the valley was opening now, the craggy little ruins of Castell Dinas Brân above Llangollen clearly visible, and the hills of Wales stretching away behind. Signs indicated that the towpath across Telford's great aqueduct of 1805, Pont Cysyllte, was closed. Never believe a sign until you've seen for yourself. It wasn't:

We went along it. The height was awful. My guide, though he had been a mountain shepherd, confessed that he was somewhat afraid. 'It gives me the pendro, sir,' said he, 'to look down.' I too felt somewhat dizzy, as I looked over the parapet into the glen.

Thus George Borrow, in 1854, having been told by his guide that 'it's the finest bridge in the world; and no wonder, if what the common people say be true, namely that every stone cost a golden sovereign'. Nowadays it's less the stone piers that impress than the cast-iron work, in the use of which Pont Cysyllte was a pioneering structure. I've no engineering knowledge, but to pick up on and wonder about detail such as the diagonal jointing in the canal trough is both satisfying and teasing, an entrant and aesthetic clue to a world turned technological. And so we went quietly on, keeping to the towpath of the Llangollen Canal now as it flowed – this feeder canal has a remarkably swift current – through attractive meadows, past cattle drinking places and under sturdy bridges with worn stone steps, to reach Llangollen as the lights of the town were coming on and the Sunday visitors were departing. We eased into the Bridge End Hotel to drink a pint or two of a beer of which old George would surely have approved. It felt like Wales again. It felt like coming home. And I thought to myself that there are few things so calming as sitting with a good friend over excellent beer at the end of an interesting day, with the better half of whatever journey we are on still ahead of us.

May: In Edeyrnion

Our road wound along the banks of the river Dee, which falls murmuring over its pebbled bed at the foot of the mountains, whose steep sides are covered with wood of the largest growth, here and there the shaggy rock, more than half concealed by the surrounding foliage, peering its broken summit beyond the most extended branches, and threatening, by its fall, to obstruct the course of the river beneath; whilst the spreading beach-tree, and mountain ash, that are found in great abundance on its banks, dipping their slender branches in the stream, and above all, upon the lofty summit of a conical mountain, the castle Dinas Brân, rising in ruined majesty; at once afford an interesting spectacle of grandeur and sublimity, as well as of beauty and cultivation.

Thus wrote Joseph Hucks, touring on foot through north Wales in the summer of 1794 with the poet Samuel Taylor Coleridge for companion. The Romantics loved the environs of Llangollen, and so do I. It's a bustling little Victorian town that shrugs off its own shabbiness and delights in its situation, clustered around its high bridge over the river. More than any of the other settlements throughout the Welsh Marches, it has a sense of being the gateway to Wales. The Welsh border may be a few miles to the east, but suddenly at Llangollen all the elements that define Wales coalesce. The castle Hucks mentions is so sentinel and native to the place, craggy and ruined yet dramatically defiant. White tiers of cliff layer the bluffs to the north and the westering sun tints them red. Weatherbeaten faces still give voice to the old language of Britain in pubs and shops. In one past dimension of time that these streets inhabit, gipsy-loving George Borrow, with his shock of white hair and his suit of broadcloth in dusty parson-black still strides loquaciously and interrogatively about, garrulously overbearing towards most whom he meets. A century later, Dylan Thomas strolled through:

> You could be in any Welsh town on any windy snip of a morning, with only the birds and the river fuming and the only brightness the numberless greens and high purples of the hills. Everything is very ordinary in Llangollen; everything is nicely dull, except the summer world of wind and feathers, leaves and water. There is, if you are deaf, blind and dumb, with a heart like cold bread pudding, nothing to remark or surprise.

The river announces its departure from the hills by a froth and a leap over the town falls, just below the bridge and under the big bay window of the Royal Hotel, in which time-hallowed and fading establishment it's long been my habit to stop for coffee before setting out into the hills. One fine May morning I met my oldest and dearest friend Tony Shaw here, and we lounged into red velvet armchairs to drink pots of strong black coffee, catch up on each other's news, and plan the day's itinerary. We weren't as well entertained as Hucks and Coleridge had been in 1794:

> . . . by a celebrated Welsh harper, who tuned his strings to so Orphean a measure, that a crowd soon collected round the door of our little inn, some of whom began to dance after the rustic fashion of their country; the simplicity of former times struck forcibly upon my mind, and brought back the pleasing recollection of those happy ages, when riches and luxury had not corrupted the heart of man; but when all mankind were brothers, and the interest of one became the interest of all.

I wonder if many of the products of Eton and Cambridge – as Hucks was – would these days give voice to those sentiments? I warm to the idealism – abandoned too soon by most of them, Hazlitt being the honourable exception – of the Romantics. And in clear spring weather at Llangollen, among the crowds that throng the place, it's easy to imagine that an element of it still obtains in the human spirit, however jaundiced a view experience may have brought of this latter. It was playtime, the bank holiday weekends rolling through in quick succession, and the people were out in the sun and out to enjoy themselves. We paid our breakfast bill – Borrow would have called it 'a trifling sum' – for copious draughts of coffee, mountains of thick, buttery toast, the solicitous ministrations of friendly, funny waitresses, and free copies of the *Daily Telegraph*, and were free to make our way over the Dee bridge and turn up the road by the taxidermist's shop.

We loitered outside this latter for some time, peering at barn owls and tawny owls in glass cases, a fox under a globed cover, badgers and stoats, a magnificent raven on a perch. I'd mentioned this to Jan Morris a few days beforehand whilst being shown her collection of stuffed owls, had even been wondering whether or not to buy it – something she'd insisted I do. I have a passion for ravens. Bernd Heinrich's books on them are some of my favourite reading, and Wales, my own country, has the highest-density population of them in the world. In one house where I lived the young ravens from the nest a hundred yards over the hill at the back would fly down to take food from my hand. But looking at the stuffed bird now, it inspired in me an intense, atavistic dread. How could I co-exist every day with something so hypnotically preserved in death, so majestic and fierce and bright? I reared a tawny owl once and re-integrated it into the wild. Its presence in the room where I worked was curiously disturbing. Sometimes it would float across soundlessly from its perch to settle on my shoulder, nibble my ear and shit down my back. Eventually, after I'd taught it to hunt, it graduated into trees farther and farther from the house, coming back to feed less frequently. But still at times I would see it in the woods, where it seemed once more appropriate. Interesting how uneasily the wild sits with our home environment, as though its emblematic power calls up something unquiet in our own spirits that can only be appeased under open skies.

Tony tired eventually of my gawping, open-mouthed fascination, and dragged me away, up to the towpath of the Llangollen Canal. I cannot believe that there is any better exit from a British town than the towpath of the Llangollen Canal. For these last two miles of its brief length, the canal is narrow, fast-flowing, pellucid. Trout of some size lurk in its weeds, and proud, noisy flotillas of ducks and ducklings navigate its surface, scolding with much indignation at the horse-drawn pleasure craft that dawdle up and down. Walk it in the afternoon and it's a thoroughfare for people, chattery-merry and bright-faced, coming down from the hills. The Dee rushes through its gorge, at times so narrow it seems almost jumpable, the stepped strata through which it cuts creating standing waves where the canoeists play. The canal is fed from a beautiful little weir, the

Horseshoe Falls, constructed by Telford, above which is a long, still pool overlooked by the old church of Llandysilio. We paused by the pool to exchange pleasantries with a stern and attentive goose that was standing guard over two sleeping ducks, before branching away from the river to walk a mile along a lane to the little village of Rhewl.

From the woodland of ash and oak along the bank to our left came the drumming of great spotted woodpeckers – an evocative sound that is actually the expression of territorialism and not a search for food. From time to time we'd be vouchsafed a glimpse of one, but these pied and gaudy birds, scarlet at nape and rump, are very shy. An occasional group of walkers strolled along the road, chaffing us in the familiar manner of the community of the outdoors about the pub that lay ahead, urging us to hurry before their ilk had drunk it dry. In Rhewl itself, we came across the Conquering Hero Community Centre. Why so called, I enquired of a group of people standing outside?

In the dulcet tones of mid-Lancashire, from a man with his leg in plaster back came the reply. That in the old times there'd been a hero . . .

The old times? Oh yes – a long time ago. He'd conquered summat round 'ere. Welsh, most like. 'Don't be daft,' his companion – a large, florid woman in turquoise-and-tangerine cotton print – told him, kicking the side of her foot none too gently against his broken leg, 'it used to be a pub, that's all.' But no longer? No – that was down the road, and we'd best hurry, else it'd be drunk dry.

It was a hot day. This warning was becoming a refrain. We injected some urgency into our progress and hastened past a red-brick chapel from the Methodist Revival with a Ferguson tractor of a date nearer to that time than ours and with a hessian sack across its metal seat parked outside. Before long we arrived at the Sun Inn. It was cool, empty, stone-flagged and staffed by a witty barmaid who doubled as the village postmistress. She soon reassured us that there was no danger of the beer running out. That, of course, gave us latitude to sit in the garden in the sun, and in order to avoid dehydration drink a pint of it, followed by

another for purposes of comparison; and because in George Borrow's day we would anyway have called for a quart of foaming ale for each of us at the outset, before writing a literary classic at inordinate length, much of which is given over to discussion of the quality of the same:

> Tom . . . returned in a twinkling with a tray on which stood a jug filled with liquor and a glass. He forthwith filled the glass, and pointing to its contents said:
>
> 'There, your honour, did you ever see such ale? Observe its colour! Does it not look for all the world as pale and delicate as cowslip wine?'
>
> 'I wish it may not taste like cowslip wine,' said I; 'to tell you the truth, I am no particular admirer of ale that looks pale and delicate; for I always think there is no strength in it.'
>
> 'Taste it, your honour,' said Tom, 'and tell me if you ever tasted such ale.'
>
> I tasted it, and then took a copious draught. The ale was indeed admirable, equal to the best that I had ever before drunk – rich and mellow, with scarcely any smack of the hop in it, and though so pale and delicate to the eye, nearly as strong as brandy.

The beer Tony and I drank in Rhewl may not have been the cowslip-wine-with-overtones-of-brandy variety formerly made by Tom Jenkins in Bala, but this pleasant interlude afforded us opportunity to study the new map I'd bought in Llangollen that morning, on which, to our amusement, we discovered a new symbol – a pint pot, half-emptied.

Between us at the Sun Inn, and Corwen – not many miles distant but an increasingly likely candidate for today's ultimate destination – there were several more of these symbols on the map. One of them was even on our side of the river. It gladdened our hearts. The Vale of Edeyrnion, as this stretch of the river's course is called, was becoming an increasingly happy, holiday choice of route. And it is extraordinarily lovely – the river hidden away from the main Holyhead road as it curls round spurs sent down from the heather-and-bracken hills to the north. By flower-banked lane and riparian footpath, we strolled into the heat of the afternoon. From the farther bank came the jewel-glint of a kingfisher. By Cefn y Coed the buzzard wheeling close above our heads was, we suddenly realized, no such thing. Its forked tail and colour proclaimed it to be a red kite. Across the river, tree-crowned, was Owain Glyndŵr's mount, in the place from which he took his name. At Fronlwyd, on the wire of a fence, trapped and desiccated corpses of moles were displayed – poor warning to these blind creatures, and a barbarism distinctive to this area. I had a flashback to first encountering it one late October half-term forty years ago, walking this same riverside lane with a schoolfriend, David Bates, bound for the youth hostel at Cynwyd on one of my earliest visits to Wales. Memory is so vivid, so arbitrary in its visitations. Joseph Hucks, with whom we started this day, had something to say on that subject too:

Memory backward turns her view, and assimilates the objects before her, to some certain passage of our life, that impresses upon the mind a shade of melancholy or joy, according as those passages have been marked with pleasure, or with pain. It is not therefore that there is any absolute impression made upon the mind, from the scene before us, whether it be bright with sunshine, or overcast with clouds, but it is memory which associates to some event, or transaction of former years, which, though scarcely perceptible, is the cause of such an effect.

I remember how I felt, remember my state of life, on the long-gone day when I first saw mole corpses on the wire. Affect from that time haunts me still. How will I feel, if I survive another forty years and pass this way again, about this present phase of life, this upriver pilgrimage away from compounding and destructive anguish back to a significant source? At neat, Victorian-villa'd Carrog we drank more cooling beer on the terrace of the Grouse Inn, and watched holidaymakers splash in the shallows of the river. A fisherman cast his fly upstream of the old bridge, which we crossed to gain the former railway. It leads now as a green track shearing through a spume of thorn-blossoms on either side into the centre of time-abandoned Corwen, and our day's journey's end.

June: Faultlines

What is it I wish to express? Intense appreciation of the beauty of sun and sky, and earth, and the feelings that come from them and from the leaves and flowers: not the rational part so much as the pure soul part: how do this without prayer or autobiography?

Richard Jefferies, *The Story of My Heart*

In shimmering heat of the greenest month, after the idyll of a weekend's reunion with my companion, I sat one Monday morning at a plastic pavement table outside the Central Cafe in Corwen, pondering the day ahead. I have a considerable affection for this little grey stone town, strung out along Telford's Holyhead road, squeezed in between the Dee and the slatey bluffs that rise to the high Berwyn moorland beyond. It's unpretentious, workaday and a little down-at-heel, like an old craftsman existing on an inadequate pension. I've been passing through here and relishing its individuality for as long almost as I've been going into the outdoors.

So I idled over coffee and toast and poached eggs. I read a newspaper and watched the place going about its daily routines: delivery men rattled trays and hastened away in a slamming of van doors; ancient, tottery ladies bought little bags of vegetables and chattered with a quick, sun-warmed gaiety; tie-dyed women of a certain age who'd drifted in decades ago, lured by cheap property and unhurried ways, who'd green-fingered their roots into the local soil and stayed implanted themselves after their broods of children had left, made comments on the weather in practised and minimal learners' Welsh to old men leaning on sticks beneath the recently-erected comic-grotesque statue of Owain Glyndŵr – the greatest of Welsh warrior-heroes, and reduced by this supposed tribute to the status of a fork-bearded, wellington-booted, malignant, ill-proportioned and supplicant dwarf. I've been told that from time to time in the dead of night the statue's taken away and cast into the river. Whatever loyal faction of the local community does so, does right. It should be left there to wash downstream into England.

I found myself thinking of the memorial to 'Che' Guevara in the Cuban provincial town of Santa Clara. It's cast in the same metal as this pathetic figurine, but the statue of Che is majestic, dominant – a Christ-militant figure, surveying the landscape he liberated from a mighty plinth friezed around with scenes from his victories. You can thrill to memorials like that. They suggest their object was worth celebrating. Why cannot this old, small country liberate its imagination and accord Glyndŵr one on that scale? To this folly in Corwen, so ill-judged and marring the town's pleasant little square, the fitting response is to shake your head and hurry on your journey.

I did precisely this, by a narrow street that climbs to the west from alongside the churchyard, where my companion and I took our first walk together. That was on a hard-frozen day of December, with a lancet wind blowing. I remember picking up a worm from the frosty grass by the path, warming it, feeling it stir before I lifted a sod and put it in the unchilled earth beneath. Succoured in a safe and caring place, things live and thrive.

The street drops down after half a mile to a road heading west, south of the Afon Dyfrdwy (once at Corwen, to refer to the river as the Dee seems almost discourteous, for it flows through the Welsh heartland now). I had good reason for taking this route rather than the paths that lead more pleasantly on the farther bank of the river; but the road anyway was empty, and relaxing to walk along.

The hawthorn blossom that had been so startling in the hedgerows only a week before had died away to faded pink and khaki husks that hid tiny green carmine-blotched hips. Now was the season of the dog rose, the foxglove and the elder's flowering. I do not think there is any more lovely time than these few brief days when the dog rose blooms. Perhaps it's the ache of its brevity that enhances its beauty. Once they burst ornately from their cases, the five-starred, butter-centred flowers are so delicate in their variations of pink and white and faintest mauve blushes, so fragile and short-lived in their glory before the petals curl and dry and litter the ground. All along the roadside their long, trailing stems, wickedly hook-thorned, entwined with the dry, stick-like branches of the elder, inspiring even that unattractive tree to its own sublime display. Starry-laced, small and faintly pungent flowers exploded out into frothy flat white heads from spriggy green stems that look like scientists' molecular plans. In a kind of reverie, touching and inhaling all their scents and fragrances, I came to the stile and field path that leads down to the old church of Llangar.

Pennant barely sees fit to mention Llangar. He even places it on the wrong side of the village of Cynwyd, which suggests that he didn't visit it. Perhaps his informants had made out that it was too rude and primitive to deserve his notice. If so, then the most eminent of Welsh antiquaries was for once ill-advised. Llangar is a gem, perhaps the most beautifully situated and instantly appealing of all the small and simple medieval churches with which Wales abounds. Its walled churchyard slopes steeply westward towards the confluence of Dyfrdwy and Alwen just below. The valley of the latter leads your eye up to the heather moors of Mynydd Hiraethog. Stacked asymmetries of graves slant across the greensward under sturdy clumps of yew and ash. The whitewashed church nestles into the hill, its affecting little crude bellcote patched with bright yellow lichens. The elegant

lettering of graffiti carved into the stone of the south doorway dates back to 1617, and the wood of the door has the enduring, organic presence of material worked and re-worked over centuries by human hand. The plashing of the river over its gravelly shallows counterpoints the long, breathing peace that rises around the place.

The church, when I first walked here forty years ago, was becoming derelict, but in recent years it's been sympathetically restored by the Department of the Environment. Peering in through the windows – churches like this have to be locked these days, which is as sad a reflection as any on our times – you can glimpse medieval wall-paintings of ferocious, leaping beasts, and see box pews and a three-decker pulpit that look to date from the seventeenth century, when this now-isolated location would have been a focus for community and belief.

Since I was last here a memorial bench which must lay fair claim to being the most beautifully positioned in Britain has appeared, facing west above the church, with a plaque inscribed to John Cowper Powys. It gives the address – 7, Cae Coed – in Corwen to which he moved in 1934, and where he wrote the two best historical novels in English since those of Scott. Powys, untouched by Modernism, is the least fashionable of the great English-language novelists of the twentieth century, but he's one of the most complex and rewarding. His novels are Dickensian in length, sprawling, funny, romantic, overblown, and completely individualistic and unique. Only Hardy has an equivalent sense of the force of landscape and nature in our lives; but grim old Hardy lacks Powys's Blakeian and luminous veneration for all living things, and his warmth of understanding for human idiosyncrasy and motivation. He's one of the rare writers you come to love for the sense of their own character infusing their work. The thought of him on his daily walk visiting this quiet churchyard adds

to its attraction. I wonder how often he sat here on the close green turf, listening to the river, looking out west, silently? What conversations with those who chanced upon him, and what reflections? Did such brief acquaintance disturb the reverie, or relieve the essential loneliness, of the writer's life?

I let myself out by the lich-gate, towards which leads a restored stone avenue of contrived ancient appearance, and I turned downhill to gain the track of the old railway that used to run to Bala and beyond. It was one of the first cuts that the notorious Dr. Beeching made to the great web of British rail transport in the early 1960s. I remember travelling along this line on a hot Sunday in 1960 in one of the Ramblers' Specials excursion trains that ran from Manchester's Exchange Station. With an odd and eccentric character by the name of Len Chadwick, who wrote a weekly column under the byline of 'Fellwalker' for the *Oldham Evening Chronicle*, we toiled up

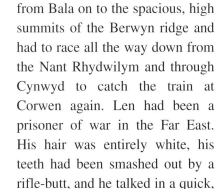

from Bala on to the spacious, high summits of the Berwyn ridge and had to race all the way down from the Nant Rhydwilym and through Cynwyd to catch the train at Corwen again. Len had been a prisoner of war in the Far East. His hair was entirely white, his teeth had been smashed out by a rifle-butt, and he talked in a quick, incessant jabber from between toothless gums. I met him when I was twelve, in a railway carriage returning from just such an excursion as this. He was poor, dirty and uncouth, worked at a menial job in the typing pool of a Lancashire cotton mill, wore rags, tied his flapping boot-soles on with string, picked up cigarette stubs from city streets and cafe ash-trays, crumbled the tobacco into a tin to roll in his own papers and smoke incessantly. He made fumbling, anxious advances to me once or twice, I slapped him away and we stayed friends. He recited endlessly the verses of Ebenezer Elliott the corn-law rhymer, discoursed on the history of socialism, would often talk in Esperanto and about the ideology of that failed universal language. Judge him as you will from this brief account – to me he was the most intellectually excited and politically and culturally informed person I had then met. Those long return journeys in crowded carriages – the gas-lamps being lit in the twilight along station platforms at Llangollen and Ruabon, conversation across all divides of gender and generation wide-ranging and intense – were some of the most educative experiences of my life. I dreamed them back into existence, and the mood of those days too, as I drifted along the quiet green way.

There is no obvious sequence of footpaths on either bank along this stretch of the river, so I thought to try holding to the old line. No doubt this involved a certain amount of trespassing, but that's an activity I've always considered legitimate, and at times have positively relished and been prepared to argue for ferociously. The weather was warm and fine, so that any farmers or bulls that I might encounter would perhaps be less aggressive than usual. And piecing together a route a hundred yards at a

across the air and herons flapped slowly toward the water. Stately progress of a slow buzzard was reduced to tumbling panic by the malicious play of a pair of ravens. A curlew circled to distract me from her nest in the rushes, calling all the while her alarm, like a doorbell with the batteries running down. The railway bridge over the river ahead had gone. Instead I followed footpaths into Llandrillo, where young women teachers, fecund sensuality of high summer upon them, laughed and conversed with farmers' sons over the playground wall, half an eye on their charges all the while and their whole biology focused on choosing a mate with whom to breed their own. Men on ladders whitewashed cottage walls, and the village pub was shut.

There is not the same holiday feel along this stretch of the river as in lower-down, more popular Edeyrnion. This is a local place, of summer fairs, church fetes, gardening clubs, rural transport schemes and meetings of the Tibet Society of the United Kingdom. I hurried through, high hills breaking the horizon now to the west and a steady burr of tractors thrumming from the hayfields. A polecat emerged from the undergrowth to lope and loop along the grassy verge. These strikingly attractive large weasels seem not so numerous in Wales as they were twenty or more years ago. I recall a friend of mine hearing her baby cry indoors as she worked outside her house of Isallt Fawr in Cwm Pennant in the mid-1970s. She went inside to find a pack of polecats in its cot, attacking it. Just beyond the culvert down which the polecat disappeared was a lane, and a sign for 'Branas

time is a good metaphor anyway for the conduct of one's life. I amused myself as I strolled along and surmounted the occasional barbed-wire fence by expanding that conceit. At one point a pool of quaking green slurry in an old cutting barred my way and caused me to skirt wide. By Cynwyd, beneath the medieval bridge, an old couple bathed, drifting through the arches on water of depth and power, debris piled against the stone piers. This whole valley is a major faultline that runs from Tywyn on the coast, through Bala and on into England, the river following it as faithfully as our emotions channel and flood through the weaknesses of our character.

In the water meadows ringed plovers scattered pealing cries

Isaf Personal Development Centre'. I turned down it, wondering who assesses what constitutes development in personality at these places, by what codes do they judge, to whom do they report, and how 'developed' are the assessors' own personalities? I have a no-doubt-wholly-uninformed suspicion that these institutions are on a par with those so-called 'adventure' centres, where what's on offer is no more than sensation, illusion and thrill.

Across Pont Cilan I climbed back on to the old railway and careered along, a flock of gentlemanly rams penned into a small enclosure and a huge, phlegmatic and benign South Devon bull providing diversions along the way, to the Bronze Age chambered cairn in the meadow below Tynygraig. It's ringed with gnarled hawthorn, its covering mound of stone mostly levelled, but three massive uprights still stand, radiant with mystery, visible for miles up- and downriver in this wide and beautiful valley. Pennant, though fascinated generally by what he considered 'Druidical reliques', again missed them, his eye fixed too firmly on the hillside above, which he describes in close detail:

> The road runs at the foot of a brow, of a stupendous height, covered with venerable oaks, which have kept their stubborn station, amidst the rudest of rocks, which every now and then shew their grey and broken fronts, amidst the deep verdure of the foliage of the trees, which so strangely find nutriment amongst them ... The whole scenery requires the pencil of a Salvator Rosa; and here our young artists would find a fit place to study the manner of that great painter of wild nature.

At Llandderfel, its church also being locked, I missed out in my turn on the chief relic of the place – an odd wooden carved animal called Ceffyl Derfel, which in fact is a headless stag, remnant of a much larger carving, to which folklore and some authentic history attaches. Here's Pennant's account:

> The church... dedicated to St. Derfel Gadarn... was remarkable for a vast wooden image of the saint, the subject of much superstition in ancient times. The Welsh had a prophecy, that it should set a whole forest on fire. Whether to complete it, or whether to take away from the people the cause of idolatry, I cannot say; but it was brought to London in the year 1538, and there used as part of the fuel which consumed poor friar Forest to ashes, in Smithfield, for denying the king's supremacy.

On the village's main street, whilst I looked at the map, a man, bare-chested in the baking sunlight, hailed me in a Scottish accent:

> 'You lost then?'
> 'No – just looking for a pub.'
> 'It's across the bridge, and it's shut.'
> 'I'd better go to the Post Office then.'
> 'That's shut as well till three.'

He shot me a rueful grin as I headed away up the hill to Bala, thoughts firmly and thirstily fixed on the last stage of this journey, to the river's source.

July: The Source

. . . hydromancy still remains practised among us; of which I shall have occasion to speak of more than one kind.

Thomas Pennant, 1781

The cockney accent of an old woman sounded strange in the context of a Bala cafe, like some familiar garden plant found in a wild setting. In her seventies, alien and lonely here, she made little conversational sallies to a group of solid Welsh women at the next table, who received them with slight and sidelong inclinations of their heads. She wore a jacket even in this hot weather, to cover up her skinny arms she told them. They pursed their lips, leant back, folded bare and ham-like forearms, hands tucked behind them so they seemed twice normal size. She had cried all last night over the little murdered girl in Sussex whose body had just been found. The women raised their eyes and looked beyond each other's shoulders, discomfited. The minister on Sunday had reminded of how the Bible demanded an eye for an eye, she continued. The women lowered their heads and shook them in saddened incomprehension. 'What must the little child have suffered,' she concluded, gathering up bags and shuffling away to catch a bus, leaving behind downcast faces, pained silence, a clamour of unspoken, decent guilts dragging barbed hooks across their consciences.

Bala is traditionally like this – intense, moral, communitarian and somewhat apart. I walked up the medieval borough's tree-lined central avenue and took a riverside path that leads out to Pont Mwngwl-y-llyn at the north-eastern end of Llyn Tegid – the largest natural lake in Wales. Oddly situated among houses, there was a glimpse of Tomen y Bala, the tree-covered castle mound that in Pennant's day was 'in the summer time usually covered in a picturesque manner with knitters, of both sexes and all ages' – the former cottage industry of Bala having been the manufacture and export of stockings. On this hot, busy day it was deserted.

The four-mile length of Llyn Tegid offers little in the way of options to those who don't like walking the roads. I could have

joined holiday crowds on the lakeside railway, but that didn't appeal. So instead I marched, as George Borrow had done after a breakfast of 'pot of hare; ditto of trout; pot of prepared shrimps; dish of plain shrimps; tin of sardines; beautiful beef-steak; eggs, muffin; large loaf, and butter, not forgetting capital tea', on a 'gloomy and lowering' morning a century-and-a-half before, down the verdant little road undulating along the south-eastern shore.

Llyn Tegid means 'beautiful lake', and it is that. The name suits it far better than the prosaic Bala Lake which precedes it on the Ordnance Survey map, or the archaic Pimblemere which that displaced. It's rich in a folklore of drowned villages, wicked kings, harpists who escaped through the virtue of their muse, strange fish, waters that flow through the lake without ever mingling. Its vast framing of high hills and wide purple moorland open to the rain-bearing winds made it, before water management schemes were implemented, exaggeratedly variable in its level. When gales raged along its south-west/north-east axis, floods were annual and commonplace, its river, the Dyfrdwy, seen as a capricious and powerful deity. 'Bala Lake . . . is wont to rise at times from seven to nine feet above its normal level,' wrote Principal Rhys in his magisterial *Celtic Folklore* of 1901; 'The inundation which then invades the valley from Bala down presents a sight more magnificent than comfortable to contemplate.'

William Bingley, a century before Rhys, was even more dramatic in his description:

> . . . when the winds rush down from the mountains . . . they drive the waters before them, even over the great part of the Vale of Edeirnion, rising in stormy weather very suddenly from the joint force of the winds and mountain torrents, sometimes eight or nine feet in perpendicular height and almost threatening the town with destruction.

Dyfrdwy translates as 'water of the divinity' from old Welsh, and lent itself to Deva – the Roman name for Chester. Milton refers to its 'wizard stream' in *Lycidas*, but the veneration of the river preceded his date. Pennant tells of its being 'very prevalent in the time of Gildas, in the Sixth Century, when our ancestors strongly retained the idolatry of the Druids among their Christian rites'. Whether you call it Dyfrdwy or Dee, it's safe to assume that this river was one of the oldest, most primitive of British gods, far pre-dating Christianity.

My road, for the four miles to Llanuwchllyn at the south-western end of Llyn Tegid, was curiously untravelled. Not a car passed, not another person was to be seen. When Borrow, fuelled by his gargantuan breakfast, came this way he had the company of a boy in a long white greatcoat with a dog called Toby. The boy related the legend, by which Borrow was much taken, of Old Bala, drowned because of its wickedness under the waves of the lake, the water washing the place clean.

Immediately after the boy leaves him, there occurs one of the most telling passages in all Borrow's writings – one of those illuminations that raise an author irremovably into our affections:

> . . . a small delicate furred creature with a white mark round its neck and with a little tail trailing on the ground ran swiftly across the road. It was a weasel or something of that genus; on observing it I was glad that the lad and the dog were gone, as between them they would probably have killed it. I hate to see poor wild animals persecuted and murdered, lose my appetite for dinner at hearing the screams of a hare pursued by greyhounds, and am silly enough to feel disgust and horror at the squeals of a rat in the jaws of a terrier, which one of the sporting tribe once told me were the sweetest sounds in *natur*.

The animal would have been a stoat – still plentiful in the Welsh hills, creamy-bibbed and their coats chestnut-rich in summer, going into ermine in winter. Warmed as much by Borrow's words as by the day, I ambled down into Llanuwchllyn and drank a pint of good beer to honour his memory in its happy, welcoming Welsh pub, The Eagles.

The way on from Llanuwchllyn follows a complex sequence of footpaths south of the Dyfrdwy to cross the main Dolgellau road, and then the river itself by some massive stepping stones at Rhyd y Brain – the crows' ford. Beyond them an old track, its exposed bedrock scored by iron-shod wagon wheels, climbed up to the moor. It would all once have been spaciousness here, but a blight of conifers has spread across it. Soon they will be cut down, the thin and unprotected soil washed out in the rains of winter to be deposited in Llyn Tegid. According to Pennant the lake was 'forty-six yards deep, with three yards of mud'. The forestry contractors will do their best to reverse that equation. There was a sustaining way of life and a community here, which economics and profit have defeated and destroyed. 'We intend to plant 800,000 acres in Wales,' a government spokesman stated after the Second World War, 'We intend to change the face of Wales. We know there will be opposition but we intend to force this thing through.'

Under the dark blemish of these trees were viable farms, bought by compulsory purchase from those whose families had owned them for generations. 'It's not true that only poor land was used,' the poet Nesta Wyn Jones, who lives six miles to the west across the hill, told me. 'They planted on hayfields where I used to play as a child.' She went on to show me an old photograph of the family round the hearth at Tŵr y Maen, just beyond the ridge ahead of me. I recalled for her the description by Patrick Monkhouse of meeting the farmer there, when he crossed this great tract of wild land in the early 1930s:

> Tŵr y Maen is one of those remote Welsh farms which pick up an inconceivable living under circumstances which would drive the average Englishman crazy in a month. The farm is linked to the world by a rough cart-track. Two miles down the valley is the next farm. In about seven miles it leads to a main road, not near anywhere in particular. If the farmer sees a strange face once a week, he must take a lot of time off. This does not, however, depress him at all. As we drew near, he called out to us, 'Good day! Fine day! Ever been here before?' as if there were so many people passing that he really couldn't remember whether he had set eyes on us before or not.

'That would have been Ifan, the last of the brothers,' Nesta explained, 'Here he is, see. He died in Wrexham.' For many in these Welsh heartlands, that old and prosperous town of the margins had a grim resonance, the lure of its industry and work dragging their roots out from the old life. In so many dimensions – emotional, spiritual, physical – this land is soured by loss, broken connection, exile: 'I do not think there is any occupation . . . as favourable . . . as that of those who dwell on the land and obtain their living out of it. In this work one has to do daily with one's fellow creatures, man and animal, and with nature herself in every aspect. From cradle to grave, the inheritors of the earth are in closest touch with all the secret powers of life,' wrote D. J. Williams in the great Welsh prose classic *Hen Dŷ Ffarm* (*The Old Farmhouse*). Today, dispossessed, we are hard-pressed even to begin to define his meaning as we falter towards it at the urging of instinctive need.

My track reached a shoulder of the moor, and scattered stones of a Bronze Age settlement where the sense of overlay through millennia was powerfully present. I headed for a sheepfold at the edge of the forest, to enter which I had to cross the Dyfrdwy again. It had become a peat-brown and tumbling mountain stream. I followed a firebreak into the trees, picked up a forestry track, and trailed along that to a ford, the spruce thick and silent around me. But the act of walking itself in these last stages of the journey had become a balm and relaxation. I looked over a tumbled wall that had defined some former boundary lost now in the forest, and met the gaze of a young, gingery fox – so vividly alive in that dead place it seemed like some lesser deity. It sensed danger, bounded away to its earth among the roots of a fallen tree.

The river led me out from the dark wood. Tiny brown trout flicked and darted in its pools. Streamside vegetation, combed one way many feet above the water, testified to recent floods. It emerged on to the most tussocky, sun-blazed, fly-plagued, boggy moor I've ever had the misfortune to cross. Drainage ditches were concealed under the bleached, dead grasses, adding to its stumbling torture. The few patches of drier ground were the province of tormentil, thistle and rush. Clumps of shrubby cinquefoil in flower gilded the morass. Ground like this depresses you, the stink and stain of its hidden pitfalls, the distance and uncertainty of objective grinding like antagonism in a marriage at whatever pleasure and confidence the day may bring. On Carreg Lusog a moss-topped upright railway sleeper, its pitch-pine splintering and exfoliating in wind, sun and rain, stood sentinel against an outcrop, unwittingly memorialising the more recent of former ways in the valley below.

The stream jigged along, defining the forest boundary on its farther side. Without any semblance of a path to guide me through its infancy, at every fork I chose now to follow the tributary of most substance. Where the line of trees cut north, the Afon Dyfrdwy curved west and headed into the face of Dduallt, which has long been my favourite Welsh hill. Its name means 'the black height', and it rises abruptly from a tawny

moor and the flatness of a great marsh. More of the inquisitive-shy foxes haunt its summit, ready to take food from you. It is as good and lonely a viewpoint to all quarters, along many perspectives, as any in Wales.

The infant river had dwindled by now to the tiniest of rills, at times a hand's breadth across, at times not visible but only audible as it gurgled under the vegetation. Miniature pools were starred and braided with water forget-me-not, and coltsfoot bristled from the banks. I came at last to a boulder hard under the face of the mountain, and beneath it was what seemed to be the last pool. Hot and weary, I took off my rucksack, washed the salt sweat from my hands and face and looked around. The words of a simple, resonant poem by Raymond Carver were running like water through my thoughts:

> Can anything be more wonderful than a spring?
> But the big springs have my heart too.
> And the places streams flow into rivers.
> The open mouths of rivers where they join the sea.
> The places where water comes together with other water.
> Those places stand out in my mind like holy places.

The river flowed away to find its path through the marsh, to join with other streams and rivers and come into its strength, into its broad mature channel, its valleys and meanders that I'd followed through difficult long months all the way from the estuary and the sea. I watched its indissociable substance self-renewing, setting out with fresh purpose every moment. The day was very still, the only sounds in this quiet place of the mountains those of water and the chipping insistence of a stonechat among the rocks.

A deep, rolling call came from close behind. I looked round to see a raven ten yards away, watching. It launched into the air and climbed powerfully to soar away behind the summit ridge. There was something odd about where it had perched. I looked closer, saw stone piled on stone, an apex wall. I crossed sodden ground

to it. On the face of the mountain above, gleam of water on bare rock and the heather blooming. At the exact point where the ground levelled was a small, rough building, west to east in its orientation, the east end a massive boulder the shape of which echoed the apex wall to the west. Lichens thickly encrusted its three built walls, oak fern swayed from crevices and the marsh vegetation within had absorbed space. But beneath the great rock, flowing out of this ancient chapel, was the first water.

Why should I – other than that there is no mention that I know of it, no mark of it on any map – have been surprised to have found at the source of this holiest and most lovely of Welsh rivers a shrine? Sanctuary at the river's source has been a tradition, a necessary and primal belief since the birth of religious wonderment. Here, how could it not have been observed? For us, struggling through our own morass of sensation, obsessing around self-affirmation through power, image and material wealth, having subjugated yet not propitiated its god, what can a place like this have to offer, what role can its tutelary spirit play in our lives? Why had I been impelled to come here?

Jung wrote that 'before the Christian Church existed there were the antique mysteries, and these reach back into the grey mists of neolithic prehistory.' He went on to suggest that: 'Mankind has never lacked powerful images to lend magical aid against all the uncanny things that live in the depths of the psyche.'

'Never before lacked,' he should have written, for he went on to protest against what he termed 'the alarming poverty of symbols that is now the condition of our life'.

Maybe to follow the river from its sea to its first spring is as good and therapeutic a primal symbol as we can still possess: to hold to its course; to endure whatever travail we encounter in that purpose, and the water's periodic raging; to seek out beyond all polluting unkindness both in others and in ourselves its source, and to find there what there is to be found? In doing so, there is just a possibility that we can objectify our own states of being, regain the celebratory glory, and, reaching beyond fear and all its masked demons, come to terms at last, come to understand. And then, perhaps, we can re-make, learn to relate, gain that patience that enables us better to comprehend and endure. Re-integrated, the possibility of renewal thus glimpsed, we can follow back downstream; joining those with whom we should rejoin in this heartening flow, that may once again become pure, may once again – though differently – be revered, no matter whether as love or nature, wisdom or the godhead, or the literal river. Like the river itself, the flow of love can be endless, self-replenishing, protean in its capacity to re-shape and return to its object.

Can it also heal?

There are situations all of us encounter or create where it seems that the best we can expect is to outlast the worst others may inflict, caring for them come what may, continuing to hope that they may somehow, from some unaffected part of their

being, accord in whatever faltering measure with something of the same faith. And sometimes, through our own vulnerability, we quail, cannot even sustain our accepted role, and hence fail the hurt and incapacitated ones whom we love as they insist everyone will and must fail them. Sometimes, too, we see with shocking clarity that for those (for us?) bewildered and made fearful as children, in continuing anger and fear, to receive love is the greatest difficulty. Yet surely, beyond all echoing curses, in some guise love can flow on, permeate, ameliorate?

I dipped my hand into the pool and drank, crossed myself, blessed those whom I love and those whom in fear and angry reaction I have hurt and hated too, left a gift to the raven on the chapel's topmost stone, and went my way, thoughtfully, not without hope, not without self-reproach, across the wide moor.

Epilogue: Epiphany 2001

. . . it is when you come back at nightfall, and look in at the familiar room, that you find Love or Death awaiting you beside the stove; and the most beautiful adventures are not those we go to seek.

Robert Louis Stevenson, *An Inland Voyage*

Every lonely river must go home to the sea. I make my annual January pilgrimage to the westernmost point of the region that has long been my home – to Ffynnon Fair beyond Uwchmynydd, holiest and most elemental of all our holy wells. Traverse of the slant ledge to its purpled recess is perilous in a dying storm. I study the waves that sluice up the channel I must cross. Timing is everything. A heavy, cross-shaped wedge of wood that's been cast in the sea – a notice or a sign – is sucked out into the sound and scoured away; and so will I be, if a wave catches me.

In a rush I'm across, spray slapping at the rock wall I've traversed, draining down it in streams of lace. I lower my head to the well-water, liquid light in its trinity-shaped basin, a smooth untaintedness to its taste. I have known those who would not drink, for fear, or from suspicion that it, filtered through these oldest, farthest rocks, might be polluted. I say a prayer here, not from my own need but for the welfare of others and for the right gravity of friendship, and return to the safe rocks.

Sea-swirl and sound and the white foam, 'so arrogantly pure a child might think/ It could be murdered with a spot of ink', and the glittering path of the sun softening the outline of a jag of ruins on Ynys Enlli beyond – do all these lovely, intangible things give the lie to the framing around me, that's fractured and rough? The salt-rime of the fretted rock that stings as it cuts, the dynamic thick impasto of the sea as it mutters against these same rocks, 'love is thus, love is thus – harsh on the surface, spirit-born, transcending all contingencies, of limitless depth . . .'?

I find it wholesome to be alone the greater part of the time. To be in company, even with the best, is soon wearisome and dissipating. I love to be alone. I never found the companion that was so companionable as solitude.

Henry David Thoreau, *Walden*

For now, that suits. This progress over many months has given me that strength again; and perhaps, through long reflection, I can bring it home at last to you, my love? The sky above is a faded blue, too pale yet for the stars, and right for the ending of a journey. There are none here today but ghosts and memories, if I wished to call them up for company. But, kind or angry, blaming, unwitting or sad, I do not. I desire only the peace of communion, of oneness with the world, that comes with grace momentarily at times like these, and in the heart through good faith may endure. God is love, love is god, and lives as source of all our best somewhere in each of us.

Faith expresses a relation from personality to personality.

Søren Kierkegaard, *Journals 1853-1855*